Infidelity in Marriage: A Complete Self-Help Guide to Rebuild Relationship & Recover from Pain

How to Rebuild Trust and Save Your Marriage after Wrong Decisions and Infidelity in Marriage

By: Paterson Keith

GW00383044

Infidelity in Marriage

Publisher Notes

Disclaimer

This publication is intended to provide helpful and informative material. It is not intended to diagnose, treat, cure, or prevent any health problem or condition, nor is intended to replace the advice of a physician. No action should be taken solely on the contents of this book. Always consult your physician or qualified health-care professional on any matters regarding your health and before adopting any suggestions in this book or drawing inferences from it.

The author and publisher specifically disclaim all responsibility for any liability, loss or risk, personal or otherwise, which is incurred as a consequence, directly or indirectly, from the use or application of any contents of this book.

Any and all product names referenced within this book are the trademarks of their respective owners. None of these owners have sponsored, authorized, endorsed, or approved this book.

Always read all information provided by the manufacturers' product labels before using their products. The author and publisher are not responsible for claims made by manufacturers.

Table of Contents

Infidelity in Marriage

DEDICATION

This book is dedicated to Jimmy, who made this book possible in many ways.

Introduction

When infidelity in marriage breaks lose...

Perhaps the most painful experience within a marriage is infidelity. Unfaithfulness breaks a partner emotionally, and surviving it is a must. Statistics show that 50% of marriages experience unfaithfulness, which means the greatest pain in marriage is experienced by at least 1 spouse out of a hundred marriages.

Attraction

Physical attraction is usually the start of everything. Attraction is sparked from someone you know well or someone you spend most of the time each week, like in instances of co-workers or even just friends. Affairs are even harder to illustrate, but it happens when husbands lose interests in marriage or wives feel abandoned and left out.

Ending an Affair

Ending an affair at the earliest possible chance is best, but avoiding attraction before an affair even begins is better. However, when a person is already in the attraction stage, it may seem to be a magical potion that lures one closer to infidelity. In some cases, affairs come to an end with a simple confession. It may be difficult for some, but it works for many.

The Unfaithful partner

So what if you are in the shoes of the spouse whose partner was unfaithful? What do you do? Is it easy to forgive, forget, and go on with life like it never happened? Sometimes when a spouse finds out that a partner has been unfaithful, it ends up in separation (worse scenario maybe divorce), especially when the lover is still in the picture. Other spouses value the vows of marriage; they still find it in their heart to forgive and forget for the sake of the children, however, the trust is no longer as good as it was.

Understanding the spouse in pain

After everything has been said and done and forgiveness takes place, everything may seem to be back to normal but actually not. Memories can still haunt the relationship, but there are ways to impede bad memories, so that it will not be a factor to destroy a marriage in recovery.

Rebuilding marriage

Are you ready to restore marriage? Where do you start? Are there rules to follow? Restoring a broken relationship and rekindling love within is a challenging task which requires husband and wife effort. Sure there are rules, but it really comes from both parties; how they will handle the situation and how they will embrace each other in marriage again.

Infidelity is indeed an experience that is devastating. However, many couples are able to grow out of it and tend to rebuild love, relationship, and friendship. How do they do it? Marriage counselling, books, psychiatric help, and many more similar methods—these are third party interventions that can help husband and wife recover. Is it effective? It can be effective when you allow it to be effective but can turn out not effective if you impede the regrowth of the relationship.

There are many ways to provide help in infidelity, however, everything really happens based on how the receiver of help useses it. Usually the one in trauma is the hurt spouse, and dealing with infidelity can really be one hell of a time that can affect everything and everyone involved. And it is most saddening when children are involved.

CHAPTER 1
-
How to React To an Affair?

So you have all the evidence to prove that your spouse is cheating on you. What should you do? Of course, you feel hurt, betrayal, and all of sorts of agonizing pain.

You want to know the truth but you are not sure where to start. You want confrontation but you are not sure if it's the right step.

Handle the Affair with an Open Mind

When you find out your spouse is cheating on you, your initial reaction of course is anger, denial, hatred, and then the question why. After your spur of emotions subsides, you then think clearly and make plans how to confront your partner. However, you are not sure what to do, and needless to say, how to confront your spouse.

If you are a woman with a cheating husband or a husband with a cheating wife, there are important things to consider doing the right action and not regretting it at the end. Whatever decision you have in mind right now, it is important to manage the situation, so that it doesn't go out of hand. Here are 5 important things you learn to help you through the situation:

1. Do not leave your spouse yet or even try to put him out of everything

Leaving your spouse should always be the last resort. For now, you should keep a close eye on what they are up to. There are many things to know to keep you and even your children's security intact, so keeping them close is essential. Note down everything in a journal. You may need it someday. Also, the chances of working out things in the marriage are highest when you are together.

2. Keep your husband's or wife's infidelity issues in secret

You would need someone to confide to in severe situations like this. However, be very careful as to who you share it to. Sometimes, the person you may be confiding in is the third party involve. It is also a bad idea to confide to the opposite sex. More often than not, sharing confidential things may also spark something in between, so you should not choose a friend of the opposite gender to confide in.

Confiding in your partner's family also may not work. For all you know, they may have known about the affair before you knew it. Not even a good idea to tell your family about it. Sometimes, they react more aggressively than you do. So it may be best to keep it to yourself, or to tell someone whom you really trust. Sometimes, professional help can be the number 1 person to turn to.

3. Denial of the affair is not a good action

Do not pretend that it is not happening. Denial can only make things worse, and you do not want that to happen. You have to face reality and at some point let your partner know that you are aware of what is going on and that the affair has to stop. The earlier you let them know, the better. Affairs lurk in the dark and just the simple fact of letting your partner know can put a stop to it.

4. Before confrontation, have a proof, a plan, and a purpose

Experts agree that confrontation is imperative when cheating is involved. However, a plan is important. Confrontation would require you to choose the right time and the right place. Cheaters always use lies, so it is not really a good idea to just ask 'Are you cheating on me?' You will get a big "NO" for an answer.

The very best approach you can take is to present the evidence—names, phone calls, times they meet, places they go, people who knew about it, etc. The right questions to ask after evidence is presented are: why, how long, is there love in the affair, and now that you know about it, what is next? Then listen.

The answers you get are important for you to assess where your marriage is at and for you to make the right decision.   The lesson here is never ever confront your spouse about cheating without concrete evidence.

5. The third party is not worth your time

Do not be obsessed about the third person involved. It is a totally waste of time. Besides, you wouldn't want them to feel that they are the "better" part of the game. While there is a part of you that wants to unfold the other person involved, it is not really a good idea. Dragging the person's name into the picture just focuses on the third person and not on the real issue.

Here are reasons why confronting the "lover" will not do you any good:

- Avoid humiliation or any frustrations by making unnecessary phone calls or confrontations.
- Harassment or threats will just put you in a bad light and may not be a good thing in the eyes of the law.

17

- Name-calling, belittling, or criticizing only puts your spouse into their defense.
- Obsession towards the third party will only make the affair stronger.

Are you going to end up wrecking your marital relationship, or are you going to save it? The end result relies on the manner you take care of things when you initially found out about your spouse's affair. In this initial phase, you may be unclear of what you're going to do. Yet at the very least, you understand how you should deal with matters before it goes out of hand. So whether you decide to stay with your partner or just leave them, knowing how to handle matters allows you to make wise decisions in the future.

A Word for the Unfaithful

Have you been unfaithful? Open your mind and read this.

Consider what statistics show
The possibility of an effective relationship that has rooted from extra marital relations does not even come close to one to a hundred. A marital

relationship that begins in unfaithfulness has no real foundation. You enter it with sense of guilt, embarrassment, depression, fear, and everything that comes along with that. In addition, the continuing battle of child custody. So is your extra marital affair worth it?

Think about your children

When there are children and you are being unfaithful to your spouse, your kids will certainly suffer the situation. You are actually contributing to turning their lives upside-down by destroying the peace and harmony in the home. Have you thought about how the courts will look at you as a parent? You may not have thought about it, but in divorce, children are always in play. And infidelity in the midst of divorce can put you into a bad light and make you lose the children as well. So think about it.

And if you are having an affair with a married person, what gives you right to destroy such a wonderful family and put innocent children out to suffer the consequences of it, all because of your lustful needs?

Start being honest with your partner and especially yourself

When you engag in an affair and your spouse finds out about it, will you be willing to end the affair? Do you still have other matters to hide? The truth will set you free and your way to rebuild a relationship that you have tarnished. If you are not able to get out of the affair, you may need professional help.

Take responsibility of your own actions

It is your responsibility to let your spouse know and be honest on the reasons that pushed you into such a relationship. If you are really sorry about what you did, do whatever it takes to earn that trust again. And really be sincere about it.

Take time to assess your commitment in marriage

If you are committed enough, then work on rebuilding your relationship. Behave the way that is expected of you, and do whatever it takes necessary to avoid that wrong path again.

CHAPTER 2
-
Facing the Consequences

Financial worries, health concerns, and arguments about your kids can put strain in the marriage. These are a few marital issues that cause heartache as well as devastation. However, it is infidelity that shakes the foundation of marriage that may lead to break up and separation.

However, not all marriages really break apart after infidelity. There are marriages that survive infidelity. Time helps heal the wounds, and with proper thinking from both parties, there can be a mutual agreement to stand strong and stay together for the sake of the family.

Defining infidelity

Infidelity has been given a lot of definition, however, it boils down to one single factor – that is unfaithfulness that breaks trust and confidence in a relationship. Affairs that lead to infidelity are usually a product of fantasies—an escape from reality filled with marital issues.

Why affairs happen

There are many contributing factors to infidelity. Sex is just a related factor. Main factors that have the most weight are individual differences, low self-esteem, insecurities, bad habits such as alcoholism and even drugs and sex addictions.

Marital issues come with marriage and family. As the family grows, so do the marital issues. This build up in marital issues can fuel an affair quickly, like an escape goat from the real thing.

Triggering factors that lead to Infidelity

- Physical and Sexual attraction are common reasons for partners to go astray instead of suppressing the feelings
- Confiding your marital issues in the opposite sex other than your partner such as colleagues, friends, and even mentors

The Consequences of Unfaithfulness

The most obvious consequence of unfaithfulness is broken relationships. When a partner breaks the bonds of marriage and resort to infidelity, trust is marred and honesty can never be the same again. How do you think the faithful would partner feel? We are just human beings. Upon finding out about an explicit affair behind your back, you want to let go, and you are left hurting and agonizing in pain.

While many relationships are left broken with infidelity, there are more negative consequences to it:

Infidelity Harms the Self Esteem

The person that has actually been ripped off by cheating will certainly suffer damages to self-esteem. Usual thoughts of self-questioning, "Am I not good enough" and if-only, I-should statements can be haunting and really leave a person really sickened from the brain down to the heart.

In the same manner, children tend to have the tendency to take all the blame for the breakup. Sufferers usually condemn themselves for the reality they are going through. But then again, the choice of cheating was not yours, and in the middle of marital problems, the cheating was still beyond your control.

Trust becomes a difficult subject
There will be an issue on trust. The partner who had been faithful will find it difficult to ever trust again and may doubt his/her judgment on other people. And when the time comes to end the relationship and begin a new one, the fear of infidelity can be great. It is then necessary to take care of these trust issues, even if it implies seeking the help of a professional.

Having a sense of instability
When infidelity and unfaithfulness comes in to the picture, it's like the whole world comes shattering into pieces and that sense of security has been disturbed and broken. It is in this time that survival

skills are needed. Let the past remain in the past and continue moving on, especially if children are dependent on the strength that one parent still has to keep the family intact.

Emotional instability

After all the pain and heart ache, it is natural that you will feel all kinds of emotions from crying to screaming, anger, and hatred. It is important to sort these feelings and work through them. If you need to talk through what you are feeling, talk to a friend or a family member who can understand you. Sometimes, professional help can help a lot.

Experience the Ripple Effect

Unfaithfulness could create a ripple effect in one's life. You may look at everything that surrounds you differently, from your job, your friends, and even the way you make your decisions. These changes can be either negative or positive, but one thing is for certain, it has changed a lot of aspects on the victim's life.

In times of this life changing event in your marital life, it is necessary that one need not make major changes in the middle of psychological imbalance.

Infidelity in Marriage

The effects of extramarital affairs sometimes extend to your job, your activities, and your life choices. It can be positive or negative.

CHAPTER 3
-
Recovering from Infidelity

How to rebuild a broken relationship

When a beautiful relationship is broken due to infidelity, rebuilding trust and confidence can be a great challenge. There will be doubts in between the lines, and one partner may always relive the pain and it can be a matter of continuous argument.

Before you even decide to start picking the broken pieces, ask yourself sincerely, are you serious about staying with the relationship? What provoked you to have an affair?

Your genuine and honest answer will help you decide on the next steps.

Talk Effectively

You have to make an earnest effort to talk effectively with your spouse. There are many relationships that end up in failure becaue there is lack of communication. If you're not communicating the problem or what's bothering you to your partner, it is far from possible to mend it.

Schedule an appointment

Schedule an appointment, so that you could sincerely talk. Even in the midst of a busy schedule, like work, or kids, you willl have to make time to for sincere talk. Put away distractions when you finally get your partner to sit down and talk. Take your time to communicate. If it requires the whole night, then let it be.

Talk at the right time

Do not spring a serious conversation with your partner when the time is not right. It will just end up in an argument as your partner may react defensive. If this happens, keep your calm and say,

"Can we have time to talk tomorrow? It's important. "

Listen actively

When the conversation finally takes place, listen actively. Put your focus on your partner; listen to what he/she has to stay. Let them finish talking, don't interrupt.

Choose a public place to talk

Some conversations may not go smoothly as planned. Emotions can be overwhelming and voices can be raised at anytime. Choosing the park or anywhere public can control the situation, and thus, less yelling can take place.

When you are really sorry and ready to do anything to regain trust and rebuild the family, here are tips that may help.

1. Apologize

You will need to apologize and be sincere about it. Let your spouse know how sorry you are and that you regret the fact that you have cheated in the relationship. Even if sincere apologies are not accepted the first time, try harder to gain their forgiveness.

2. Be honest

You know you've done wrong. Honesty entails admitting the fault, expressing concerns in the most appropriate manner, and being willing to accept change. It the start of a healthy relationship.

2. Stay calm

Engaging in arguments, and fighting about who is right or who is wrong will not do any good. It is best to stay calm. Take time out or sleep on it. When both of you are ready to speak over a cup of tea on a Sunday afternoon, then listen and respond appropriately.

3. Focus on yourself

You do not have the power to change other people, but you have the power to change you. You are responsible for your actions, and the changes are totally up to you.

4. Change the way you do things

It is at this time that you will need to make some changes in the choices you make in terms of behavior and interaction. Put your spouse and children in priority.

5. Let the past remain in the past

When conflict has been resolved, do not allow the past to ruin what you both have in the present. It is important to stay away from creating another trauma, and thus, refrain from re-enacting the source of conflict.

Letting go of the past is the very first thing that has to be done in order for a brand new relationship to move forward. Rebuilding a relationship takes time, effort, and participation from both parties. There should always be open communication, proper expression of emotions, and most of all, honesty.

There are many articles written about how to mend broken relationships and marriages, all of which talk about how both parties (husband and wife) should act to keep the relationship going. There is one thing missed out – Are you both still in love, or have you fallen out of love and are just keeping the relationship alive for the sake of others?

Mending broken marriages should be the effort of both husband and wife. They both should be willing to participate in the process. Without the participation of both, all will just be a waste of time and energy.

CHAPTER 4
-
Rebuilding Trust

A marriage stands or falls on the quality of its foundation. - John Townsend

Miki sits at the corner of the bed, still not believing what she has to hear. Her 9 years of marriage is crumbling at her feet. Vester has been her everything. And now, a good friend just informed her of a 5 year old son her husband has from an affair.

Hurt and confused, Miki just sits there, looking out towards the window staring at nothing in particular.

Her eyes are red and swollen from hours of crying. She has no idea how to face her husband of 9 years, but she has to confront him. She just has to know the truth.

Like many other couples, Miki and Vester are now facing a crisis in their marital relationship. That trust has been broken, and it may ruin their marriage of 9 years.

Perhaps one of the most remarkable gifts in marriage is the ability to trust your spouse, trust that your spouse will not hurt you emotionally, trust that there is honesty in the relationship, trust that there are no lies, and trust that both are only thinking of the best interest of the marriage.

Understanding the Nature of Trust

When there is trust in the relationship, there is pure security. You are at ease in many ways.

Be Trustworthy
In order for other people to trust you, you will have to be trustworthy in return. That is how it is in a relationship. There is trust because it is earned, and both parties are trustworthy to receive trust.

Put an End to Deception

Deception is the number one cause of losing trust. When you are a victim of deceit, you will find yourself hating and unable to trust that person again.

Lies have no place where there is trust. That is the main reason that trust and truth always come together. Infidelity is a product of lies that should be ended as early as possible because it destroys a lot of relationships.

Marriages that are surviving the consequence of unfaithfulness will have to learn to be honest even if the truth hurts. It is the first step to mend broken relationships.

Change is a good thing

If your marriage is going through infidelity issues, do not give up on trust. Give your partner a second chance. Learn to listen and make wise decisions after you have found out the truth.

Giving your partner a chance entails more than forgiveness and apologies. Real changes are needed to rebuild trust. In some cases, the professional intervention is needed to allow healing take place.

Trust is a fragile matter. It can break into pieces, but it can also be rebuilt.

What does trust imply?

Trust means you have confidence that someone is honest and at the same time faithful. You have confidence that they are able to keep vows and promises. Trust comes with love, acceptance, and forgiveness.

Trust is the foundation of every relationship. It is the pillar of marriage that binds a family to stay intact. Trust requires honesty, acceptance, and forgiveness. When trust is broken, there is aggravating pain that causes doubt and makes the foundation shaky where respect, love, and friendship are replaced with hatred, insecurity, and fear.

When trust is not present in the household, you may not have privacy on your phone, your emails, even your personal mail. It can be the triggering factor that may cause continuous arguments. There will be no peace inside the home.

The question is how to rebuild trust to rebuild the marriage?

1. Denying never works

Quit denying and lay all your cards on the table. Denial just worsens distrust. The truth has to come out one way or the other if you want to rebuild trust. The truth can be hurtful and adds up to the pain that is already there. And so is the healing process. But nevertheless, when everything is out, there is a chance for forgiveness.

2. Being casual, defensive or righteous is not the answer

A sincere effort is needed to bring down the walls built by distrust. It doesn't help to add in a defensive or casual behavior as it aggravates more anger and hatred, and thus, nothing can be resolved. Rather than being casual or defensive about the situation, it is necessary to show earnest sincerity.

3. Reflect on the reasons of unfaithfulness

It would be nice to hear your side of the story. Be open and introspect on the factors that made you cheat. There are many ways to discuss on the issue.

Professional help can be a good alternative to assess if you have a sexual addiction or to find out if your marriage is missing out on something that your partner fails to provide. Open communication is important, so as to prevent the same events from happening.

4. Make everything accessible
Be open to what you have. Avoid hiding things. Let your spouse know of your schedule and be where you are expected to be. Your privacy is no longer yours, but your spouse is also entitled to know everything that goes on.

5. Go through your vows in marriage one more time
Take time to out to remove the gap and restore communication. Learn new things about your spouse and let her in to your building world too. Communication is the key. Talk about what you want and what you don't want. In the same manner, listen to what they have to say.

Take note that when you decide to gain back trust, this means being open and some change of habitual activities. An open and clear relationship is important in every relationship. Time can heal all wounds, and with time, communication can bridge the gap and reunite the once happy and content couple. It is not just a matter of decision; it is a matter of participation and willingness to submit to your partner and your partner to you.

Infidelity in Marriage

CHAPTER 5
-
Effects of Affairs on Children

Infidelity can break the bond between husband and wife. And in the same manner, it leaves pain among the children.

The battle for custody alone can leave the children confused, and they may lose that trust they have built within the family circle. They learn to hate, to put the blame on parents, and may find comfort in others.

Whether or not the mother or the father is the one that has an affair, it still boils down to children being affected in this situation. If the situation goes out of hand and separation is the solution, then the children are the most affected. Even if it is handled in the most discrete manner, it still has a great impact on the children.

Common reaction of children towards Infidelity

Embarrassment

Children whose parents are going through the issue of infidelity are often deeply shamed by the situation. Infidelity is a big no-no in society, therefore, children feel embarrassed about what their parents are going through.

Confusion

Parents impose rules, and when these rules are broken by the parents themselves, children get confused. Is it okay for adults, particularly parents to break rules? At this point, children find reasons to break rules in school or in the society and will try to get a way with it as a result of confusion.

Anger

A usual reaction from children is the feeling of anger towards both parents. The unfaithful parent is very easy to blame. Children are easily outraged and easily shut out the parent. The faithful parent, on the other, hand is still blamed for not doing anything to prevent the break up.

Distrustfulness

Children develop distrust when a parent betrays the whole family. Children will tend to build their own world, away from the hurt and pain, not trusting anyone that comes even close. They develop a sense of insecurity as a result of boken family ties.

How to Help

Although parents cannot undo marital issues, especially when it has come to the point of separation, parents can help children going through these insecurity issues with the help of therapy. It is important to make some time for them just to listen to their emotional needs.

It is at this point that despite marital diffrerences, parents come together to talk about the welfare of the children. The child needs to hear an explanation that is why it is important to have the child understand what parents are going through.

It is important to let the child know that even if parents have come to the point of separation, the relationship between the parents and the children has not change, and they are the most wonderful thing that happened in the relationship.

What are the steps that parents have to take in order for the children to understand infidelity issues?

In the event of infidelity, it is just right to let the children know about the issue. Infidelity does not only affect the couple but the family as a whole.

Steps couples can take to lessen the pain of infidelity among children:

- Opening up to your children and being there to answer their questions can help lessen the pain of the situation.
- Open communication gives an honest dialogue between the parent who had an affair and the children.

- Open communication helps in the healing process of the family unit and provides lessons that needs more understanding.

When is the appropriate age to talk to children about infidelity issues?

It is important that the children will have some kind of understanding about why mom and dad are talking abou this matter. Letting the children know at the earliest possible time is better.

When you know that your child is already able to interact, then it is a good idea to talk about the situation in a subtle manner.

As the children grow older, parents can go into more details, so that they can understand.

Who breaks the news to the children?

Ideally both, mom and dad have to be present when disclosing infidelity matters to children. The person who has caused infidelity should be the one to initiate the conversation, and the partner cheated upon should be present to show no defeat on the situation.

This is important, so as to leave a good lesson to the children. To see that the other spouse is strong enough to accept the situation makes the children learn to accept and understand better too. At the same time, the children are not left to blame either party for what their family has become.

What are the long term effects of infidelity among children if the situation has not been disclosed?

When the situation has not been disclosed to the children at the earliest time, and when the children find out later on, there can be a feeling of betrayal all over again, like it has happened yesterday. In this case, further explanation may be needed.

CHAPTER 6
-
How to Forgive and Forget

Why is it hard to forgive?

One of the reasons most of us resist forgiving is a lack of understanding. We cradle pain, and it fills our hearts leaving no space for forgiveness. We think we understand forgiveness, but in most cases, we really don't.

Forgiving does not mean that everything is okay. Trust is not regained just by forgiving.

The very first step to understanding forgiveness is by defining what it is and what it is not. And then, you can allow youself to forgive and forget while learning from it. When you forgive, you don't free a person from the responsibility. You should still hold the person accountable of his /her actions.

How to Forgive and forget

"Let go of the past hurt and mend broken relationships" - Sarah Neish
A psychotherapist, Emma Baskerville says – You can forgive someone even without understanding the reason why they caused you pain. Sometimes, asking for an explanation why they hurt you does not make sense. When you ask why and what you get is "I don't know", it just makes things worse and leaves you irritable.

A positive first step is to say 'I don't know why you did that, but I can accept that it happened and try to move on'.

But when you go, "I really don't know the reasons why you did what you have done. I can't undo that but to accept it and move on." With this phrase, you are opening a conversation, encouraging the person to talk and at the same time, they are forgiven, but it doesn't mean that everything is over.

Accept their apology

At the height of your anger, you may not find yourself ready to listen to any explanation or even accept an apology. Let that hurt emotions come out and then calm down. Let time pass, and when you are ready; accept their apology without any suspicion.

Learn to let go of blame

Forgiveness is an agreement between 2 individuals. One vows not to repeat actions that have caused pain, while the other accepts and leaves everything that has been done in the past.

Work out through differences along the lines of marriage without constantly referring to past mistakes. There may be a triggering point somewhere that will remind you of the pain, but it should be dealt with properly without blaming anyone.

Learn to Open up

The most difficult part of forgiving your spouse from the faults of infidelity is the risk that you will have to go through the same pains again in the future. 'Vulnerability can make a person feel really fragile and weak, but it is also the way to intimate relationships that provide security. We need to open up in order to get close to people, so try not to put up barriers when you've been hurt.

Four Barriers You Must Face To Allow Restoration of Relationship

It is important to understand these crucial concerns to help you get through the recovery process

To victoriously journey on the road of reconciliation, the couple must surpass 4 essential barriers. If a couple is making the effort to restore a relationship after infidelity, they will most likely deal with the same barriers. Consciousness and understanding of the trials that lie ahead may be the first step toward restoration.

Barrier #1: Wrong Thinking

Many of us inaccurately believe that adultery is merely a misguided action; however, it is a violation of God's heavenly order for the sanctity of marriage. An indvidual who previously had an affair needs to seek their partner's forgiveness, not alone for the adulterous way, but as well as for violating the sacred commitment of marital covenant.

An intact marital union generates a feeling of trust and security to be able to give one's self freely to your partner. A restored sense of security and trust brought about by asking and obtaining forgiveness for destroying the covenant can start to reestablish joy, confidence, and peace.

Barrier #2: A Multi-Faceted Struggle

It is worthwhile to comprehend that a wounded partner, will battle with several concerns. The sexual identity is now baffled. The act of immorality will make the grieving party ask deep in her soul, what appears to be wrong with me that he may desire somebody else?

Another highlight is the trouble of pity growing inside. Self pity that he would want another woman. Yet, another area is confusion over the lack of peace with one's self. Although the act was forgiven, there is a process to eventually forgive the ways that one has been impacted by the violation of their marital vows.

Barrier #3: Getting to the Real Problem

On the outside, it can look like one's behavior is the issue, and swearing "to change" is the answer. Nevertheless, the actual dilemma is in one's mind; he granted himself consent to ruin his marriage vows. To focus solely on his ways and forget about this matter of consent will leave the couple in limbo.

Overlooking the real issue can make the couple feel that there is still something wrong and no one will understand it. They will walk with difficulty, pondering the reason why their partnership is so temporary and far.

Barrier #4: Inability to Trust or Be Trusted

This is in close connection with Barrier #1. If a sacred marital covenant has been broken, trust will be the hardest—but essential—to rebuild. The meek acceptance of one's inability to handle his own mistakes or addiction to the pleasure of sin or fulfill promises is also the exact point where one can accept God's saving grace and empowerment to make a choice differently.

A partner should be able to exude humbleness and dependency to God, so the other partner can start to trust again. As restored trust develops, the couple will certainly experience abundant intimacy, true satisfaction, and continuing joy.

By fighting these obstacles with each other, wounded partners can conquer the damages of unfaithfulness. By realizing to have confidence in God in a new, much deeper way, they can take pleasure in a better, more rewarding relationship.

Comprehending Forgiveness

"Love is the union of two good forgivers." -- Ruth Bell Graham.

There will always be unexpected events wherein couples may encounter something that will remind them of what they went through. And if it happened some years ago, the wound will somehow feel fresh. Both parties will feel uneasy. It is important to discover how forgiveness really works. The "feeling uneasy" part everytime they would come across a familiar scenario would be wiped out.

Forgiveness is complex, both in serious circumstances like this as well as in the each day instances that bother our married lives.

We commit errors, and even worse, we're typically in refusal of our transgression or too arrogant or stubborn to accept it. It's an awful day at the office, or you're going through PMS, and our tempers flare at the smallest trigger of irritation.

Our partner retaliates with indignation, and the scenario amplifies. Who's at fault? Who needs forgiveness? Who admits to being wrong? Point the finger at each other, but "she started it" or "he insulted me" turns into a chant. We're equally fallen life forms. We all fail.

Recognizing our shortcomings will help us possess the grace to ask and give forgiveness. Both parties need to ask and both need to forgive, with the eager understanding that maintaining a forgiving marital relationship can stop the resentment of accumulated offenses that gradually harden hearts and create walls.

Sometimes forgiveness is not that simple

A young couple tied the knot when they were just students, and despite busy schedules, the young wife expects that they spend quality time together. Instead, the young husband spent many nights in bars drinking with male friends. When she grew angry, he accused her of pressing and trying to control him. Their words dug in, penetrating deep and hurt each other. In less than a year, they split up.

In some cases, forgiveness feels unachievable. However when we have been significantly hurt, the concept of forgiving may feel as if we're being obliged to rip our hearts out and give out to the very people who trampled it. So either we provide a perfunctory, "I forgive you," while still having the bitterness in our hearts, or we harden ourselves and physically or emotionally walk away.

Through these particularly hard circumstances, we occasionally place an unnecessary load on ourselves. Perceiving that to forgive, we must entirely forgive and get past it instantly.

Forgiveness is often a procedure, not a one-time gesture.

Although it comes down to the decision to forgive, it might take time before the heart totally accepts what the will has started. The length of time it takes may be influenced by the severity of the pain of the transgression, and we must give ourselves the grace our healing demands as we move ahead to full forgiveness.

When we've been intensely wronged, something inside yearns for justice. If we don't forgive, our desire for justice evolves into revenge, subjecting us to the bondage of anger and self-righteousness. When we decide to forgive, the justice we look for is for the other individual to experience our discomfort.

A husband that listens without getting impatient or defensive makes forgiveness became a mutual endeavor of grace. A heart of forgiveness can expand, and the transgressor forgave a period of scab-picking relapses, and together, they can move forward to a complete healing and be able to bring the process to a close.

Real forgiveness occurs when we release our hurt and dismiss it, recognizing that our husband or wife is a fallen human being, who is possibly carrying out the best he or she can with the minimal resources in their emotional, relational, and spiritual stockpile.

When we fasten our hearts on the rock of God's love, the forgiveness of our partner allows us to release our pain into God's healing hands. As grace shatters the danger of rising bitterness, it plants the seeds of a more cherished partnership. Husband and wife encounter the rejuvenating rush of independence and the capability to completely love.

Infidelity in Marriage

CHAPTER 7
-
Moving Forward after Infidelity

Regardless if you have strayed or cheated in your relationship, what matters is how you managed and moved on.

Was your partner unfaithful?

For the partner who was cheated on, it is vital that you move forward after all the aches and pains; learn to live life and love again. When you learn to trust again, then it is the key to reliving life and moving ahead one step at a time.

It is always better to live a healthy life alone than to be with your partner and stay constantly sick and stressed. You shouldn't be the one to leave. Let your partner leave. When your partner decided on an affair that just means that he/she has decided they wanted out. So open your doors to freedom.

In the event that you partner would like to be back in the home, it shouldn't be as easy as re-opening the doors. He/she must show that he/she deserves to be back in the home. Communicate your way through the relationship. Is it worth it?

There may be a point in your separation that you decide that you are better without the other then your partner or rather ex-partner has the right to know. Again, communication is essential at this point to put a closure into the relationship legally and emotionally.

Did you have an affair?
When you've decided to enter into an affair, you must be responsible of your actions. What has been done cannot be undone. But you can make a decision that can change the life of everyone involved forever.

It is not fair to make a comparison between a really new, exciting relationship to one you have actually been in for many years, where there are little ones, bills to pay, a house to manage, and even noses to wipe clean. That is a ludicrous comparison to make.

To fix your marital relationship, communication with "the other individual" should be totally cut off One Hundred Percent. You cannot work on handling the effects of the affair while you are still in it.

You need to rely on your intelligence and logic to know exactly what the appropriate step to make. Do not depend on your heart for your decisions.

Starting a new relationship when you are in a relationship does not work. So when you are already in this situation, it is either leave the marriage and free your partner or make a commitment to stay.

Be responsible to help your partner get pass through your unfaithfulness.

If you are in a marital relationship, you have a responsibility and commitment that goes beyond what feels excellent. Be at the right mind to accept that life is not just about you and what you feel is exciting at the spur of the moment.

When you decide to stay and find it in your senses that what you did is wrong, then you have to help your partner have an emotional peace. It is your responsibility now to go the extra mile to gain her trust.

When everything is said and done and you want to come to a closure, here are helpful tips on dealing with the consequences of infidelity.

10 Tips on Dealing with the Consequences of Infidelity

1. The marraige is over – Accept that fact!
Just let go and move on. Do not cling on the past. It will just remind you of the pain. Rather, look into the future where you can live life the way you want it. No more worries of demanding husbands or nagging wives.

2. Let the emotions out – Don't shove it away!
Scream if you have to, cry if you have to, and curse if you have to. Let it all out in one blow. Relieve your

heart of the pain and empty your brain of the memories. After all the hurting, now allow yourself to be at peace. Be mindful of what you allow in your thoughts. Think of the better days ahead.

3. You're scared? I know and it's normal!

Anxiety that comes after separation is normal. You should be! We are human beings after all. But never ever let anxiety overcome your personality. Rule over it. Face your fears and the road ahead will be clear.

4. Accept yourself!

No one person is perfect. Each one of us has our own flaws, and we have to learn to accept that. Instead of living in insecurity, relax your mind. Go out and feel how it is to be single again. And if the children are with you, you've got to have a good time. Your children need a break too.

5. Deal with anger constructively.

There will be a moment in your own time that you will feel the anger all over again. Face it, deal with it. So long as you are not hurting anyone, then it's okay to let it go. Seek help if you must; find space to release your anger.

6. Be true to yourself and to your friends

You do not have to hide what you are going through. Talk to friends; when they ask you how you feel, tell them constructively what you are going through. You do not have to let them pity you, let them know you just need to talk. You know you need to stay sane.

7. Open your hear to forgive

Forgiveness is more for your own good than to the other. When you learn to forgive, it unlocks the doors to a whole new world of peace and serenity.

8. Make a positive progress everyday

No matter how small it is, that still is progress that shows you are moving on towards a better life.

9. Have long term goals for yourself.

Where do you see yourself 5 years from now? For sure, you wouldn't want to see yourself living in the past in 5 years time. Picture yourself in a happy state, enjoying what you have without worries.

10. You always have a choice.

Life is a matter of choice. There is no such thing as you are left with no choice. There is always a choice, a choice to live, a choice to laugh, a choice to forget, and a choice to move on.

Infidelity in Marriage

Conclusion

In today's society, infidelity posts as one of the major problems in marital relations. And since unfaithfulness is considered as a taboo, couples shy away from addressing the issue.

More often than not, couples grow a distance without attempting to resolve the issue or to talk about the reasons why one partner is pushed into such a situation.

With open communication, forgiveness, and understanding, there is always a big possibility that relationships can work out, rebuilding the marriage in renewed vows.

Infidelity is an issue that can hurt not only the spouse but also friends and family. Children can be severely affected that can push them to go astray of the right path. And the results of infidelity can leave an overwhelming effect on the child's life.

The guilty spouse is as badly hurt too, just as the suffering spouse. Infidelity is the result of wrong decisions and temptations. And if couples have not yet recognized it, infidelity is the result of lack of communication, neglect, and irresponsible behaviour.

While there are many reasons that can cause infidelity, there are also many reasons to survive infidelity, to forgive and forget and to pick up pieces. When communication cannot resolve the issue and couples have fallen out of love, it is still possible to part as friends, especially when children are involved.

In most cases, professional intervention is the best approach to help relationships marred by infidelity.

When couples cannot resolve issues on their own, professionals can help go through the situation. Marriage counselling can even be a good alternative to work things out.

Separation or the extent of divorce is not always the solution to infidelity. When matters are complex and family and friends are hurting, the best person to help in the situation is a third party intervention.

So if you are in this kind of complex situation, it is best to stay calm. Accept the pain, acknowledge the truth and think straight. Communication is the key, and forgiveness is the door. And if you have unlocked all doors and found love can no longer be found, there is still another door to friendship that can embrace understanding and spare the innocent.

Infidelity in Marriage

ABOUT THE AUTHOR

Paterson Keith has been working extensively with young adults as well as their families and is also a motivational speaker on different facets involving state of mind, individuality and development among kids and teens. An organizer and staff to the dialectical behaviour therapy (DBT) program specially organized for young adults who are showing risky behaviours that may harm themselves and the type of borderline personality traits.

Lightning Source UK Ltd.
Milton Keynes UK
UKHW021422071218
333634UK00011B/458/P